California Missions

This book features the photography of
James Blank
and
Robert D. Shangle

Statue of most reverend Junipero Serra at Mission San Juan Capistrano.

Concept and Design: Robert D. Shangle
Author: Barbara Shangle

Third Printing, July, 1999
Published by American Products Company
6750 S. W. 111th Avenue
Beaverton, OR 97008

ISBN 1-884958-29-X

Mission Chronology

#1: <u>Mission San Diego de Alcala,</u> 1769
↓

#2: <u>Mission San Carlos Borroméo de Carmelo,</u> 1770

↓

#3: <u>Mission San Antonio de Padua,</u> 1771 → #4: <u>Mission San Gabriel,</u> 1771

↓

#5: <u>Mission San Luis Obispo, de Tolosa,</u> 1772
↓

#6: <u>Mission San Francisco de Asis</u> (Dolores), 1776
→ #7: <u>Mission San Juan Capistrano,</u> 1776
↓

#8: <u>Mission Santa Clara de Asis,</u> 1777
↓

#9: <u>Mission San Buenaventura,</u> 1782
↓

#10: <u>Mission Santa Barbara,</u> 1786

↓

#11: <u>Mission La Purísima Concepción,</u> 1787
←|

↓

#12: <u>Mission Santa Cruz,</u> 1791 → #13: <u>Mission Nuestra Señora de la Soledad,</u> 1791
←|

↓

#14: <u>Mission San Jose,</u> 1797 ↓
#15: <u>Mission San Juan Bautista,</u> 1797 ↓
#16: <u>Mission San Miguel, Arcangel,</u> 1797 ↓
#17: <u>Mission San Fernando Rey de España,</u> 1797
↓

#18: <u>Mission San Luis Rey de Francia,</u> 1798
↓

#19: <u>Mission Santa Ines,</u> 1804
↓

#20: <u>Mission San Rafael, Arcangel,</u> 1817
↓

#21: <u>Mission San Francisco Solano,</u> 1823

Table of Contents

California

✝
*California
Missions*

San Francisco Solano
(Sonoma)
✝

San Rafael
✝

■ Sacramento

San Francisco ■ ✝
San Francisco
de Asís (Dolores)

✝ San José

✝ Santa Clara

Santa Cruz ✝

■ **Fresno**

✝ San Juan Bautista

San Carlos Borroméo ✝
(Carmel)

✝ Soledad

✝ San Antonio

✝ San Miguel

✝ San Luis Obispo

✝ Santa Ines

La Purísima ✝

✝ Santa Barbara

Santa Barbara ■

✝ San Fernando

✝ San Buenaventura

✝ San Gabriel

■
Los Angeles

✝ San Juan Capistrano

✝ San Luis Rey

**Pacific
Ocean**

San Diego ■ ✝ San Diego

Mexico

Introduction

The formation of modern California takes its roots from the founding of the mission system that began in 1769 in San Diego. While this is the apparent time of entry for the beginning of California, the settling plans actually began as far back as 1493 during the time of dominance of the western world by Spanish monarchs Ferdinand and Isabella. Exploration and land claims included, in part, present-day South America, Central America, and southwestern portions of North America. Sea explorations and conquests by such voyageurs as Juan Rodríguez Cabrillo and Captain Sebastian Viscaino laid claims to land that was directly part of present-day California. As years passed the Spanish government needed to maintain a protective hold on their lands and one way to accomplish this control was through land occupation.

Spain settled in Mexico and established many missions under the control of the Jesuit Order. In 1767 under the direction of the newly appointed governor, Don Gaspar de Portola, the New Spain (Mexico) mission system in Lower California was removed from the Jesuit Order, due to conflicts of control interpretation, and placed in the hands of the Franciscan Order, namely Padre Junipero Serra and three other priests, Francisco Palou, Juan Crespi and Fermin Lasuén. Fray Serra was the founder of several missions during the time of his administration in Baja (Lower) California. Two years later the padres and the governor were directed to settle the unexplored land of *Alta* (Upper) California and the history of California began with the establishment of the missions. By this time England and Russia appeared as threats to the Spanish by encroaching on the California area.

It was impossible at the time to establish residency in an unknown land using Spanish citizens. It was decided the best approach would be to create settlements through missionary efforts followed by the establishment of pueblos or towns with Spanish inhabitants. Basic rules for claiming the territory were to be followed: certain land controlled by Spain would, over a selected period of time, return to the native people; Spanish work skills would be taught to the native people; and instruction of the Catholic religion would be a part of the program. The church was responsible for the religious conversion of the people and the Spanish government was responsible for acquiring more land for the monarch.

There were a total of twenty-one missions founded in the mission chain between 1769 and 1823. Each has its own unique history that is full of excitement, adventure, hardships, and drama. Entering a land that was unexplored and encountering inhabitants who spoke unknown languages, and who maintained different values and beliefs from those of the padres and soldiers, led to fear and apprehension for all groups involved. The limited historical sketch of each mission included in this book can only whet the interest-appetite of the reader. Each mission's historical importance must be searched more thoroughly to understand the depth of human involvement.

Indeed, the influence of the mission settlements has left a strong mark throughout California and has even reached beyond the California boundaries. Architecture, language, music, art, apparel, and children's games are but a few of the innumerable reflections of the Spanish culture developed directly from the mission era.

The founding of Mission San Diego de Alcala took place on July 16, 1769, with the dedication ceremonies conducted by Fray Junipero Serra. Mission San Diego was the first permanent Spanish settlement in California and was named in honor of St. Didacus of Alcala, Spain. Capt. Sebastian Viscaino had discovered and named the beautiful sheltered bay in 1602. St. Didacus was a Franciscan who dedicated his life to religious teachings and caring for the sick. He was canonized in 1588.

The first church was located on a hilltop (currently known as Presidio Hill) overlooking the Pacific Ocean and the idyllic valley below, yet far enough inland to be protected from inclement weather. The presidio was built alongside the mission for the protection of the padres.

Missionary conversion and "civilizing" the Native Americans was a difficult task for the fathers. The Native's attitude regarding the acceptance of Christianity was anything but cooperative. Although some did join the missionary life, the majority were satisfied with their lifestyle and simply wanted the "organizing intruders" out of their land. An extensive Indian uprising took place in 1775, one year after the mission had been relocated to the valley below, some six miles inland from the presidio to protect the Indians from unruly soldiers and to improve the agricultural advantages for the mission. Father Luis Jayme's heroic efforts to calm the Indians brought about his demise. His life was the first martyred death for Christianity in California. The raid burned the tule roofs and temporary buildings and the padres moved back to the presidio for protection, where they stayed for several months before attempting a reconstruction of the mission buildings. Mission growth and earthquake damage required the church to be remodeled several times. The permanent adobe mission structure, the design recognized today, was completed in 1813 and dedicated November 12th. The ever plaguing water-shortage problem was solved by an extensive dam and water transportation system that was designed by the padres and constructed by the neophytes six miles upriver from the mission, providing the necessary irrigation and life-sustaining water.

It wasn't long before the decline of activities commenced, once immigration by outsiders began and western settlements took root. The secularization law of 1834 took control of mission property, selling many of the buildings to private citizens. The church building, which deteriorated rapidly, was occupied by the U.S. Army from 1847 to 1858, who used the main floor as a horse barn and built additional quarters on a second, upper level. Deterioration was so severe to the adobe structure that by 1931, when restoration began, only the facade of the church was standing.

In 1931 at the time of restoration, only the facade and the base of the belfry were in evidence. Every effort was made to duplicate the original church structure and belltower at the time of reconstruction.

The simplicity and beauty of Mission San Diego de Alcala is a keystone to the evolution of the California Mission charm. Its historical significance extends to each mission developed over the 65 years of mission growth. This beautiful garden provides a center for solitude, reflection and a glimpse into mission history.

The first church was an adobe structure completed in 1802. Fr. Peyri designed and supervised the construction of the second church, begun in 1811 and dedicated in 1815. This church, 138 feet long, with a narrow nave, was designed to accommodate 1,000 people. This is the church used today.

Having access to fertile soil and abundant water, Father Peyri and the neophytes developed a rich and productive mission. An aqueduct system was built to divert water from the streams to the mission grounds for drinking, cooking, industrial needs, laundry and on to gardens and fields for crop irrigation.

Mission San Luis Rey de Francia

As he cast his eyes upon Mission San Luis Rey in 1827, the traveling Duhaut - Cilly wrote, "In the still uncertain light of dawn, this edifice, of a very beautiful model, supported upon its numerous pillars, had the aspect of a palace. Instinctively I stopped my horse to gaze alone, for a few minutes, on the beauty of this sight." What an eloquent description of the grand mission.

Father Fermin de Lasuén founded Mission San Luis Rey de Francia on June 13, 1798, on the site that once had been considered for Mission San Juan Capistrano. The mission was named in honor of King Louis IX of France (1215 - 1270) who participated in the crusades of Egypt and the Holy Lands. He was canonized in 1290. When Father Lasuén dedicated the mission, the local Native American men, women and children joined in the celebration. Fr. Lasuén baptized 54 children that day and began spiritual instruction to 19 adults. The open-arm acceptance by the Indians continued throughout the duration of the 36 years of active missionary existence. Mission records indicate that during the first six months, the Franciscan padres converted 214 Native Americans to Christianity.

As with earlier missions, the padres, neophytes and workmen from other missions constructed dwellings for the padres and soldiers. The governor directed soldiers from the San Diego Presidio to devote all their efforts in the construction of buildings at the new mission. They were to follow instructions from Fr. Lasuén "without murmur at site or work with implicit obedience to Father Lasuén." Since the military and the church had not seen eye-to-eye for the past 30 years, it makes one believe that this kind of directive by the governor was penance on behalf of the soldiers for action unbecoming the military. Father Lasuén, who normally departed soon after the founding service, remained at Mission San Luis Rey for six weeks. It was his plan to develop a grand-sized mission, both in building structure and agricultural prowess, not to mention a missionary dominance.

The driving force behind the success at Mission San Luis Rey was its benevolent leader, Father Antonio Peyri. He served for 33 years. During those years, he taught and counseled the local Natives who developed into strong figures in the mission life. Mission records report that by 1831 there were 26,000 cattle, 25,500 sheep and 2,150 horses. The agricultural harvest was extremely ample, especially boasting of the 395,000 bushels of grain and the 2,500 barrels of wine. Indeed, Mission San Luis Rey had developed into a self-sufficient entity.

Secularization began in 1834. The mission's existence waned. The Indians left and the padres departed to new assignments. The lands were confiscated from the Natives and distributed among the Mexican authorities. The U.S. government returned the church building to the Catholic church in 1865. The mission was abandoned from 1865 to 1892. The Franciscan Order established a novitiate at the mission in 1892 and the mission was rededicated on May 12, 1893.

The main structured area was composed of a patio 500 feet long and 500 feet wide, surrounded by buildings and walkways. Today's mission operates as a Franciscan Seminary and is an active religious center for the community. Peace and solitude and time for reflection is ever present at the mission.

Mission San Juan Capistrano

On October 30, 1775, Father Fermin Lasuén erected a cross and dedicated the new mission. Just eight days later news of an Indian attack on Mission San Diego led to the recall of Father Lasuén and the new mission's six soldiers. All inhabitants abandoned the site and returned to the presidio at San Diego. It was a year before the padres returned, with Fray Serra presiding over the dedication on November 1, 1776. The bells used the previous year were retrieved from their underground hiding place and re-hung in a tree. The large cross was still standing. Mission San Juan Capistrano was one of the largest and most successful missions. In 1812 records indicate a neophyte population of 1,361. The fertile soil provided bountiful crop harvests of fruits, vegetables, and grains. The large cattle and sheep herds, allowed to roam the open range, flourished and numbered over 20,000. Production was strong in the making of soap, candles, leather tanning, and weaving.

The first chapel building was completed in 1777, made of adobe and reeds. By 1796 the neophyte population increased sufficiently to require a larger facility for worship. Work began on the great stone church, a magnificent edifice reaching 180 feet in length, 40 feet in width, and at the highest point, a massive bell tower reached 120 feet. Under the guidance of master stone mason Isidor Aguilar of Mexico, the Native Americans completed the church in nine years. As the bells called the devoted followers to mass on December 8, 1812, a severe earthquake struck, causing devastation and ruin to the beautiful church; walls swayed and the ceiling collapsed, killing 40 praying neophytes. The bells were silenced as were the two bell ringers. The rebuilding of the stone church did not happen. Services returned to the original adobe church where Fray Serra said mass. In the 1890s the little church was restored. It is the oldest building in California today.

The Moorish-designed water fountains provide water for the birds that live and visit in the compound, not to mention the added beauty to the surroundings. The little swallow that returns annually to the mission lives in the many mud nests located in the nooks and crannies of the buildings. During the most recent restoration work, the mud-daubed nests were destroyed by the removal of the tiled roofs, necessary for the reinforcing of the buildings against potential earthquake damage. The removal of the vines from the buildings and stone-church ruins further destroyed bird nests. The birds had no place to call home and did not return to the mission but moved to nearby shopping centers and freeway underpasses. The Preservation Society researched the problem and devised methods to entice the birds back to the mission. So to solve the problem, big mud puddles called "Swallows Wallows" were created for mud gathering by the birds and artificial mud nests were made and placed in the swallow's favorite nesting spots. When it came time for the birds to return, their favorite meal was served, Lady Bugs. Little by little the birds returned to their "home", primarily on Saint Joseph's Day, March 19th.

Restoration efforts in the 1920s became a major undertaking by mission pastor Fr. John O'Sullivan. The charming flower-bedecked mission of today has its present image due to his devotion to the restoration project. Continued reconstruction has brought the mission to what is believed to be an authentic view of mission life during the time of the early Franciscan padres.

In 1813, a year following the massive earthquake that toppled the new church, a new bell tower was erected and the four church bells that rang so loudly on that fateful morning, were re-hung and are still in place today. The bells are rung for special events.

The threat of earthquakes is ever present. Supporting structures are in place around the massive stone ruins of the big church, warding off potential damage. The beautiful vine plants creep about, hiding faults and creating beauty and charm to the entire mission.

Many of the artifacts are as old as the mission. One in particular is older: a painting, "Our Lady of Sorrow." According to an old story, this painting quelled an Indian attack when the priest displayed the image, creating a calming atmosphere among the people. The main altar, a wood carver's masterpiece, came from Mexico City in 1790. The baptismal font of hammered copper and the silver baptismal shell were brought from Spain in 1771. Many exciting historic pieces grace the church and grounds.

Mission San Gabriel, Arcangel

Mission San Gabriel, Arcangel's location met the needs of the church and those of the Spanish government. Fray Junipero Serra selected the area he believed to be most suited for the fourth mission in the summer of 1771. However, the Franciscan padres Fray Serra selected to establish the mission chose what they believed to be a better site and founded the mission on September 8, 1771.

While the local Indians were generally peaceful, incidents of mistreatment by the military caused tremendous grief for the padres. Harassment by the soldiers made Native American trust difficult to achieve and created a lasting hatred toward the military. One particular incident precipitated a skirmish between the military and Natives and led to the decision to postpone development of Mission San Buenaventura. During this time leadership was passed to Fathers Cruzado and Paterna, who developed a trusting relationship with the frightened Native Americans. Father Paterna was replaced by Fr. Sanchez in February, 1776, and he and Fr. Antonio Cruzado were the driving forces for 30 years that developed Mission San Gabriel to become known as "The Queen of the Missions."

The first mission structures were simple, made of wooden poles and reeds. In 1775, after battling spring floods and crop loss, the mission was relocated to its present site. Construction of a new church building, made of stone, brick and concrete mortar commenced in 1791 and was completed in 1806. Father Cruzado, reared in Cordova, Spain, designed the building and captured the Moorish architecture style so identified with early Spain. The church is entered through double doors at the front. The long side is designed with high rising buttresses. The current (second) bell tower built in 1823, located at the far west end of the church wall, holds six bells.

This active mission taught skills to the Native Americans, such as soap making and tallow rendering, used for making candles, both important mission industries. Four large boiler vats are still seen at the mission. Having an abundant water supply and being located in such a fertile valley provided the necessary ingredients for agricultural achievement, such as grains and fruits, as well as developing a large cattle herd. Grapes flourished and their harvest allowed San Gabriel to be a leader in wine production, producing as much as 50,000 gallons, annually.

The mission experienced many changes since the secularization in 1834. Ownership passed from person to person and deterioration occurred. Meager care was maintained. However, the church was never totally deserted as some of the Native American neophytes stayed and a secular priest (today known as a diocesan priest) came weekly to say mass. In 1859 the U. S. Congress restored ownership to the Catholic church, and in 1906 ownership transferred to the Claretian Order, who, today, care for and govern the mission. The mission still has an active role in the local community of San Gabriel, providing ministry through its churches and schools.

The long side of this church is designed with high rising buttresses, capped in the Moorish style, and the tall, slender windows create an image not seen in any of the other mission buildings. Its walls vary from four to seven feet thick. The original vaulted roof has been replaced several times, due primarily to earthquake damage in 1804 and 1812, at which time the church bell tower collapsed. Today's church is covered with a 300-foot cedar shingle roof, the newest repair completed in 1993.

Mission San Fernando Rey de España

Mission San Fernando Rey de España was the seventeenth mission to join the chain of missions and named in honor of Saint Ferdinand, King of Spain (1217-1252). Fr. Fermin de Lasuén joined by fellow priests arrived in the area and dedicated the mission site on September 8, 1797. It was not a sudden impulse to select the site, as Gaspar de Portola and Fr. Crespi passed through this area in 1769 after departing San Diego in search of Monterey Bay. Both were delighted with the amenities of the area. There was an excellent water supply (four strong flowing streams); a spacious valley (Fr. Crespi named it *Santa Catalina de Bononia de los Encinos*, St. Catherine of Bologna's Valley of the Live Oaks); and the appearance of friendly Native Americans.

Development of the mission moved rapidly. Records indicate that within two months a small chapel was built, followed by a granary, storeroom, and a weaving room. The neophyte congregation numbered 40. As the population grew, the need for larger dwellings and storage buildings became apparent. By 1807 housing was provided for over 1,000 neophytes who made the mission their home. This census was maintained for nearly 20 years. Soon the quadrangle was enclosed by additional buildings: barracks, workshops, storerooms and family dwellings. Located near the popular highway for travelers, the mission had many guests seeking shelter and food. Always accommodating, the mission erected a large building dedicated in part to rooms for guests. It also included rooms used for a chapel, a kitchen and wine cellar. This building, currently the largest adobe structure in California, measures 243 feet long and 50 feet wide.

The padres of the mission began to feel the encroachment by the Pueblo of Los Angeles. By the 1820s their missionary strength was showing diminishing returns. The previous success achieved through agriculture and livestock also began to recede. The industries in leather tanning, soap and candle production, plus many other endeavors could not be maintained. The Pueblo of Los Angeles was a ready-made market for the mission industries, but as the Indians left the mission, the work force dwindled and the pueblo demands could not be met. Mexico declared its independence from Spain and Mission San Fernando, along with the other missions, no longer received aid and assistance from the government. The 1834 Secularization Law added to the mission's burden. The Indians left and the padres moved away. The land was sold by the governor in 1846. Ironically, the governor's brother acquired part of the land.

The U.S. government returned the buildings to the church in 1861. There was nothing to restore, as neglect and looting had left ruin, save one building. That one building, identified as the Long House, had been leased or commandeered by many people: including Governor Pico's brother and U.S. Colonel John C. Fremont. It was used as warehouse space, a horse barn and even a hog farm. In 1923 the Oblate Fathers were placed in control of the mission and they began restoration. In 1971 a devastating earthquake registering 6.1 on the Richter Scale destroyed the church beyond repair. Quickly, an exact replica was built and dedicated in 1974. The more recent temblor of 1994 again caused damage to the mission buildings. Restoration is a constant happening.

When Fr. Lasuén arrived to establish the mission, the land was occupied by the mayor of the Pueblo of Los Angeles. Though quite likely not pleased, the mayor, Don Francisco Reyes, vacated the premises and the padres moved into the small ranch house. Since the land was owned by the Spanish government, complaints were not expected from Reyes.

During the mission's first seven years, three churches were built: the first in 1799, again in 1800 and in 1806. On a December morning in 1812, a severe earthquake struck, shaking the thick walls so violently that many of them crumbled. Massive thick buttresses were put into place to reinforce the structure.

Today the mission presents a strong front to the local community, providing a respite for those who appreciate the grandeur of the mission, the solitude, and the opportunity to reflect on the achievements so earned. Mission history is well recorded and provides an excellent insight into the foundation of California.

By 1809 a new stone church was built. The severe earthquake of 1812 damaged the church, weakening the entire structure. It took three years of reconstructive work to bring the mission church back to acceptable standards, and this included an immense buttress fortification to stabilize the building.

16

Mission San Buenaventura

When approval for the founding of Mission San Buenaventura was finally obtained, soldiers and their families, pack animals loaded with goods for the new mission, and priests and other officials made the journey from San Gabriel to establish the mission. On Easter Sunday, March 31, 1782, Fray Serra established his last California mission before his death.

Original plans indicated that San Buenaventura was to be the third mission, to be located halfway between San Diego and Monterey. The delay was always blamed on lack of military protection and the need for other missions. The corridor of land suitable for habitation along the Santa Barbara Channel was heavily populated by Native Americans, divided into as many as 21 villages and some 10,000 Indian inhabitants. Mission protection was vitally important.

Conversion started slowly. The Indians were satisfied with how they lived. But over time missionary success took a firm hold. Native involvement brought the agricultural success to a high peak. Many factors, besides excellent farming abilities, allowed the crops to flourish: fertile soil, excellent climate, and an adequate irrigation system. The priests and Indians built an aqueduct system and reservoir that served a seven-mile distance, providing water to a vast area. Word spread of the abundant food stuffs. Besides providing for the large mission complex, sailing vessels anchored nearby and purchased food for their voyages. Grains, fruits, vegetables, even bananas, coconuts, figs and sugar cane were available.

When secularization was declared in 1834, the mission survived the transition quite well. The pueblo, or town, of San Buenaventura had taken hold and soon it surrounded the mission, taking over much of its land. Only the church maintained its original purpose. During 1842 and 1843 Mission San Buenaventura was the local parish church. The balance of the mission holdings was sold in 1845. In 1862 the United States government returned the building to the Catholic church.

In the 1890s resident priest, Father Rubio, believed it was necessary to "keep up with the times" and proceeded to modernize the church building. The ceiling and floor were covered with wood and the interior walls were painted white. The window openings were lengthened and filled with dark-colored stained glass. All the exterior buildings were torn down to beautify the surroundings. In 1957 renovation efforts restored the church to its original pre-modernization days. The handsome wood beams of the ceiling and the strong tile of the floor were still there, waiting to be released from the wood coverings. Today's church has been authentically restored to its original form.

The mission site was placed in a Chumash Indian village of about 500 people, known as La Asuncion de Nuestra Señora. Mission shelters, a stockade and church were quickly built with the assistance of the friendly cooperative Native Americans.

Mission Santa Barbara

One of the most beautiful missions is Mission Santa Barbara, named in honor of a young girl killed by her father for not renouncing her faith. December 4, 1786, is the first founding date of Mission Santa Barbara by Franciscan Father Fermin de Lasuén. December 4th is also the feast day for Saint Barbara. December 16, 1786, is remembered as the date dignitaries attended the founding ceremonies. It was five years following the completion of the presidio at Santa Barbara that money was released by the Viceroy to build the mission. Father Lasuén selected a site high above the valley and waters of the Pacific Ocean. The land surrounding the mission was perfect for growing crops and grazing animals.

The local Chumash Indians were an agreeable people and eager to join in the efforts of the mission. The work of the missionary fathers was successful. By the united efforts of the Indians and friars, an extensive water system was devised. A short distance from the mission, the padres built a dam and a stone aqueduct. Water was used in the gardens surrounding the mission and siphoned away to a large fountain for the expressed purpose of washing clothes. The aqueduct system transported water to a gristmill to power the wheel for the grinding of the wheat harvest, to holding tanks for drinking, and to the fields for irrigation.

The first church, constructed of adobe brick and topped with a red-tiled roof, was completed in 1789. A second church was built just five years later and destroyed by an earthquake in 1812, leading to the construction of the church recognized today. This church was begun soon after the earthquake. The building follows a pre-Christian era design from a Roman architectural drawing. The large church, 180 feet long, with ceilings reaching 40 feet high, and the room width at 40 feet, was a triumph. It was completed in 1831 with one tower in place, followed by a second tower in 1833.

When secularization reached Mission Santa Barbara, it made the transfer with little incident. Constant care allowed for the lack of deterioration experienced by most of the other missions. As a parish church, the mission maintained its integral position in the community. A Franciscan friar was always in residence.

In 1925 a severe earthquake caused the toppling of the twin towers. Reconstruction took place using reinforced steel to strengthen the structures. In the early 1950s both of the towers experienced concrete deterioration but this was quickly corrected.

The construction of many of the first mission buildings used as storage units, work facilities and dormitories was the foundation of the quadrangle, now the site of the beautifully groomed area known as the Sacred Garden.

The first bishop of California was Fray Francisco García Diego y Moreno, O.F.M.,who took residency at Mission Santa Barbara in 1842. The Franciscan Order still maintains control of the "Queen of the Missions", the only mission with two bell towers.

19

Father Francisco Javier de Uría, who was presiding priest, designed the new church. The walls were very thick, five to six feet, providing stabilization against future earthquakes. Heavy pine logs were used as support beams, logged from the nearby mountains, and clay tiles were used for the roof. This beautiful, strong building, about 139 feet long, 26 feet wide, and 29 feet high stands today, much as it did on that dedication day in 1817. During the life of the mission, the *campanario* has stood strong at the edge of the church and beside the cemetery. There have been three constructed over time. The bells hanging in the niches were cast in 1807, 1817, and 1818.

Mission Santa Ines

On September 17, 1804, Father Estévan Tápis dedicated the mission in honor of a young Italian girl, Agnes, a 13-year-old martyr executed in Rome in 304 AD for refusing to sacrifice to the pagan gods. The local Indians were familiar with mission work and enthusiastically greeted the opportunity to be part of its life. On the founding day about 200 Native Americans participated in the ceremonies, presenting over 25 children for baptizing. Fathers José Rumualdo Gutierrez and José Calzada were the first presiding priests at the mission. Their first year was very busy, as 112 Natives were baptized. The neophyte population developed slowly, though steadily, and the highest census reached 768. Nearby missions provided starter seeds, farming implements and stock animals. At its height of production, grain harvests exceeded 10,000 bushels. The livestock herds reached between 9,000 and 10,000 head. The extensive harvest expected at the mission never quite reached the expectations of the founding fathers.

On the morning of December 21, 1812, an earthquake rippled the ground so violently that the church collapsed into rubble and the surrounding buildings were severely damaged. This setback was short-lived, as the padres and neophytes began work on a new church. By 1817 the new church was completed and dedication ceremonies were held on July 4th.

Mission Indians experienced constant harassment by soldiers. The soldiers were abusive to their women and badgered the children and men. The padres complained constantly, but little was done to correct the problem. In 1824 an Indian man from Mission La Purísima was flogged by a soldier while at Mission Santa Ines. The local Native Americans revolted against the harsh treatment. The Indians were armed and organized. Taking control of the mission, they set fire to many of the buildings. When it appeared the church was going to burn, they stopped the plundering and helped to save the church. The group fled and continued their revolt at Missions La Purísima and Santa Barbara. Soldiers and Native Americans were killed during these three skirmishes and several were wounded. Eventually, life settled down and the missionary achievements again prevailed.

The Natives, under the guidance of the padres, were responsible for the mission's success. They built an extensive aqueduct system that brought much needed water to the area. They developed agricultural skills and became proficient in weaving and hand crafts. Secularization lay heavily on the mission in 1834. No longer having a mission status, Santa Ines became the parish church. Parts of the buildings were rented. The Indians left the mission. The buildings deteriorated and the land was unproductive. In 1843, through a possible land-saving device, 35,000 acres were granted to the diocese for the first educational institute in California. The land happened to be at Mission Santa Ines. The college was named Our Lady of Refuge. In 1846 the remaining mission land was sold to private citizens.

The first adobe church was completed in 1805, followed by the completion of the *convento* measuring 232 feet long. With the completion of this building, the typical quadrangle was begun (the completed quadrangle measured 350 feet square). Between 1805 and 1812 the neophyte population increased and additional buildings were needed. These were built along the quadrangle area: storage rooms, padre quarters, dwellings for the soldiers and their families, dormitories and a guardhouse. Eighty small houses were built for the neophyte families by 1812.

Mission La Purísima Concepción

The Immaculate Conception of Mary the Most Pure. Mission La Purísima Concepción honors the mother of Jesus, so named by Father Fermin de Lasuén, founder of the mission on December 8, 1787.

In early spring following a rainy winter season, soldiers and workmen from the presidio in Santa Barbara journeyed to the new mission to assist in the construction of mission buildings. The Native Americans were friendly and eager to participate in mission life. Soon after the construction of shelters, many neophytes lived within the mission confines. By summer's end the padres had baptized 75 converted Native Americans, a task unheard of by some of the preceding missions.

Missionary achievement and colonization of *Alta* California by the Spanish had been accomplished by La Purísima, the primary objectives of the Catholic church and the Spanish government. A good location, excellent weather, friendly, intelligent Native Americans, and eager, enthusiastic priests led by Fr. Mariano Payeras were the ingredients used to make La Purísima Concepción a success. Suddenly, on December 21, 1812, a devastating earthquake struck, shaking and rocking the earth. Numerous aftershocks followed for several days. The new church, built very close to the major fault, fell into shambles. The walls crumbled and the roof collapsed. Heavy rains followed the quakes and just as suddenly as the earthquake struck, a violent flood of water rushed over the mission site. From behind the buildings the earth gave way, emptying a land-locked basin of water that had accumulated from the recent rain storm. Everything was lost and desperation set in to those left with nothing. With their strong faith in God, Fr. Payeras and the other devoted padres immediately took control of the situation and started anew. Within a four-month period La Purísima was a working mission again, attaining great success once more in its agricultural endeavors and livestock production. Life was good until 1823 when Father Payeras, who guided the mission for 19 years, passed away. Soldiers constantly harassed the Indians. In 1824 an incident of an Indian flogging at a nearby mission, Santa Ines, was too much for the neophytes at La Purísima. Other factors contributed to the Indian unrest: loss of livestock due to drought, raging fires that destroyed their homes, lack of much needed supplies, and the loss of their beloved leader, Father Payeras. A revolt ensued and the Indians commandeered the mission, retaining control for nearly a month. The standoff was quickly suppressed when soldiers from the Monterey Presidio arrived, killing 16 Native Americans and wounding many more. One soldier died and three were wounded.

Ten years later secularization was instituted and mission life collapsed, leaving the neophytes without support. In 1845 the entire mission was sold to a private citizen for $1,100. By 1874, when the mission was returned to the Catholic church, the entire mission was in shambles and sold again. In 1934 Santa Barbara County acquired the mission site.

With the cooperation of both the state and federal governments, La Purísima has been reconstructed and restored to represent the truest image of mission life. Exhaustive research efforts have provided exactness concerning architecture and furnishings. The detailing of wall decorations, column construction, furniture creations, garden plants and orchard trees, and much more, have been put in place. The extensive aqueduct system is again in place, providing an insight into the engineering minds who were in charge of this great mission.

Many of the buildings erected in 1788 did not last long, as materials used in their construction deteriorated rapidly. In 1802 a larger church was built of adobe and covered with a clay tiled roof that protected the mud bricks from the seasonal rains of the area. New facilities were built for the increased neophyte population, which reached a record count of 1,522 by 1804.

Success in the fields was also an attribute for La Purísima Concepción. Located in a fertile valley with abundant water, the mission grew a variety of crops, providing a bountiful harvest. The livestock herd flourished, numbering over 20,000 head of cattle and sheep, during the life of the mission.

Those early adobe shelters were prelude to larger, stronger buildings, of which today's church building is evidence, even though reconstruction and renovation have played an important part. Imagine the stalwart church with a New England-style steeple, an austere facade, and pristine-white, horizontal wood siding. This happened when a modernizing influence took over, not only changing the exterior but the interior as well. The ceiling was covered, the floor was covered, the walls were covered, two altars were added; a major change to create a parish church atmosphere. In 1920 a fire caused enough damage to the "new" woodwork that it revealed the "old" woodwork and the "old" won out. In 1934 restoration efforts began, returning Mission San Luis Obispo, de Tolosa to the grandeur of the past. Restoration is a continuing endeavor.

Mission San Luis Obispo, de Tolosa

This lovely area was discovered by Don Gaspar de Portola, the first governor of Alta California, during the summer of 1769 while on his trek from Mission San Diego in search of Monterey Bay. The local river provided a good growing area for vegetation, and a good food supply for wild animals such as bears. Yes! Bears and they were big, strong and fierce. It was a real surprise to Portola and his men who shot one of the beasts with the mighty musket and discovered that it took more than a single shot to down the animal. A frenzied flurry took place. The bear tore around and killed a horse and frightened the men out of their wits before a volley of shots killed the bear. Even so, the local Indians were very impressed with the ease the gun played in killing the bear. The bow and arrow used by the Indians lacked instant power. Food became plentiful.

A serious problem experienced by the new mission was Indian attacks. Many of the Indians were unhappy about the missionary conversions; they wanted the padres to leave. Since the Natives had plenty of food and were content with their life, they did not need the trinkets and gifts offered by the priests. In retaliation the Indians shot flaming arrows into the tinder-dry tule roofs covering the adobe shelters and this raised havoc for the security of the mission. The fires occurred several times. The resilient Franciscan padres solved the roof problem by developing a new roofing material, used extensively in Europe and previously applied to the modest adobe chapel at Mission San Antonio de Padua: red clay tiles. Soon an ingenious method was devised to make individual tiles: clay dirt, water, horse power (for mixing clay and water), wooden molds, sun power, and hot ovens, plus a lot of labor by the mission Indians. It was time consuming and tedious work, but the efforts paid off. Not only did the tiles resist fire, they gave lasting protection from rain to the adobe walls and the interior areas of the buildings. The tiles were so successful that the practice quickly spread throughout the mission chain.

Historical records support the agricultural success of the mission, not only in the cultivation of fruits and vegetables but in the production of olive oil and wine. Missionary efforts were a success also. The neophyte population increased steadily, recorded in 1804, to peak at 832; baptisms were listed at 2,074. Fr. Martinez is remembered for his influence as well as being colorful and outlandish in behavior. Even after 34 years of devotional work for the mission, the Governor in charge removed him from the mission due to personal anger. It was soon after his departure that the mission began its downward spiral towards decay. Secularization took hold in 1835. As other missions experienced, the property value plummeted from $70,000 to a pittance. In 1845 the church building sold for $570. The U. S. government returned the meager mission remains to the Catholic church in 1859.

Selecting the "right" place was another of Fray Junipero Serra's achievements when it came to founding missions in California. Mission San Luis Obispo, de Tolosa, named in honor of Saint Luis of Toulouse, Spain, was built near a fresh water stream, sitting on a modest hill in a valley of plenty, which was named Valley of the Bears.

Mission San Miguel, Arcangel

Mission San Miguel, Arcangel provides a visitor an adventure back to the very early days of mission life. When Fathers Fermin de Lasuén and Buenaventura Sitjar located the mission near the Salinas and Nacimiento rivers, northeast of Mission San Luis Obispo, they must have believed prosperity was ensured. The founding ceremonies included neophytes from nearby missions and 15 children who were baptized that day. This event took place on July 25, 1797. Immediate acceptance by the local Native Americans, being located in such a sound area, and having the government pleased with the founding made the padres' work all the more meaningful.

Buildings were erected and mission life began. By 1803 the mission could boast of achieving over 1,000 converts. The mission lands increased as well, with holdings extending the boundaries to a total length of about 50 miles. Mission ranches were scattered over the land holdings, each specializing in particular cultivations. For example, Rancho de Santa Isabel maintained vineyards, Rancho del Paso de Robles grew wheat, and San Simeon was a livestock ranch. The fertile soil near the rivers provided excellent agricultural products for mission use and for selling. Extensive aqueducts were constructed by the neophytes to channel water where it was most needed, in the fields and the mission. The success of the mission's industrial endeavors fall directly on the shoulders of two Franciscan padres, a few soldiers and the neophytes.

A fire in 1806 destroyed most of the mission buildings, including the church and warehouse structures that stored wool, cloth and over 6,000 bushels of wheat. This demoralizing event was short-lived. Other missions provided needed supplies to "start again" and within a year's time San Miguel was back to its full strength. By 1818 a new and much larger church was ready to occupy, complete with a clay tiled roof. This roof would not go up in flames as the earlier roof did, made only of mud and tinder-dry reeds. The tile roof covers 28 rafter beams, each cut from a single Sugar pine tree logged in the Santa Lucia Mountains, 40 miles west of the mission. The church interior is quite opposite in decor to that of the plain, austere exterior of the building. Vivid colors of bright red, blue, green and pink reach out from the wall paintings by Spanish artist Estévan Muñras and his neophyte assistants, completed in 1821. The paintings and decorations have never been retouched since their beginning.

Mission San Miguel was the last of the missions to be secularized. The edict was announced in 1834, but was falsely presented to the Indians earlier in 1831 by José Echeandia, the first Mexican Governor to enter California. He told the Indians they were free to leave their mission bondage whenever they chose to, but none of them left. However, over the next three years, the population plummeted and few neophytes remained at the mission when secularization did arrive. The mission enterprises ceased to exist and by 1840 the last Franciscan padre left.

For 15 years the church was unattended, open to vandals, robbers and almost any danger. The interior of the church was never harmed. In 1928 authority was renewed with the Franciscan Order who opened the doors for all who wish to enter. The successful mission only paused during its historic journey and renewed itself, continuing on today with its original purpose.

The mission was sold in 1847. The property was returned to the church in 1859. Prior to the reactivation of the church in 1878, the buildings were used for a variety of purposes: a private home, a sewing machine store, even as a tavern. Restoration immediately commenced to return dignity to the building.

The mission sustained extensive damage during the 1906 earthquake. New reconstruction efforts began in 1948, first by clearing fragmented building parts and rubble. The only remaining structures were the baked-brick arches along the front area and the face of the church itself.

The Indian *"gentiles"* Fray Serra called to on that July day in 1771 must have heard his singing voice echo throughout the hills and through the trees for they arrived at the mission compound and many stayed to hear the "word." People are still arriving to observe the beauty and reflect in the quiet solitude of Mission San Antonio de Padua.

Mission San Antonio de Padua Jolon, CA 93928, 23 miles SW of US Hwy 101 at King City

Excitement filled the heart of Fray Junipero Serra the day he hung the bell in an oak tree in the secluded valley on July 14, 1771, rejoicing with a call to *"ye gentiles"* to join him at his new found church, named in honor of Saint Anthony, who, following his death, was laid to rest in Padua, Italy. The success of the mission came quickly and endured through the mission's active life, for the first visitor arrived quietly and alone to observe the formal blessing and religious service performed by the tenacious priest. Being well received by the padres, the Native American gathered others of his tribe and brought them to the mission. This began the great missionary success so enjoyed by Mission San Antonio de Padua. Steady leadership of Fr. Buenaventura Sitjar must be explained to understand the achievements by this noble leader. When Fray Serra returned to Mission Carmel on the first of August, Fr. Sitjar was one of two priests left to build a guiding force for the Native Americans in the Valley of the Oaks, as the area is known today. Spanning 37-years of teaching, listening and prodding, Fr. Sitjar guided the Native people to perform labor skills that produced unique results. He developed an irrigation system by damming the San Antonio River, located some three miles from the mission. An aqueduct system carried the water to holding tanks located on the mission grounds, which allowed for irrigation of the agricultural endeavors. With access to water, the first water-powered gristmill was operated, along with a fountain and bathing pool. His success as a teacher is illustrated by the book he compiled that contains 400 pages of vocabulary words spoken by the local Indians. Learning the Native language enabled Fr. Sitjar to teach the Catholic doctrine to the Native Americans in a most successful way, allowing for the first Christian marriage to be performed in California at Mission San Antonio de Padua.

When secularization arrived in 1834, it wasn't long before the entire mission began to disintegrate. The Native Americans were cast out of the mission environs and pushed back to their old ways of living. Farming and livestock management ceased. In 1845 the church was listed for sale, but with its remote location and downtrodden buildings, no one purchased it. The last parish priest left in 1882 and the buildings were abandoned for many years. Abuse by the natural elements caused extensive decay to the adobe and wooden structure. Efforts to renew the old mission began in 1903 with considerable money and physical labor extended to new construction. But that was short-lived as the devastating earthquake of 1906 damaged the mission beyond repair. Bulldozers pushed, shoved and scooped through the mission area. Workers cleared and cleaned, many with simple hand brooms, sweeping old foundation floors. Today's mission is most livable and active. All modern conveniences are part of the building, just cleverly concealed so as to maintain the original appearance of this handsomely reconstructed mission, illustrating its beauty and charm. Today the mission is privately owned by the Catholic church and remains an active center of spirituality, operated by the Franciscan Order.

The first mission church and shelter buildings were modest, but with time all things became more grand. The first use of clay tile for roofing was implemented on the church in 1776, and adobe shelters were built in a systematic fashion for the neophytes. A regular compound was erected with storerooms, barracks, shops and warehouses for storage of the successful harvests and mission necessities. As years passed the church got bigger, up to 133 feet long, and the facilities at the mission improved.

Mission Nuestra Señora de la Soledad

Our Lady of Solitude so aptly identifies the lonely mission located on the flat land of the Salinas River Valley. Father Fermin de Lasuén founded Mission Nuestra Señora de la Soledad on October 9, 1791, named in honor of the Virgin Mary, mother of Jesus.

The construction of mission dwellings was slow. A year passed before a temporary church shelter was erected. In 1797 the first permanent church facility was built, made of adobe brick and covered with a thatched roof. Few Natives lived in the area. Missionary achievements were limited to small numbers.

There were many obstacles that restricted extensive growth and development. The attending priests suffered from the dampness and cold of the winter and the grueling heat and wind of the summer. Personal hardship was ever present and took its toll on the priests. Life was so lonely and unpleasant at Soledad that mission fathers requested transfers repeatedly. Over the 44 years of Soledad's active life, approximately 30 priests served the mission. An exception was Fr. Florencio Ibañez who served more than 15 years. His remains are buried at the mission. Father Vincente Francisco de Sarría was the last priest in charge. He died while saying mass in 1832, collapsing at the altar.

When Mexico declared its independence from Spain, monetary support and supply provisions ceased arriving from the government. Mexico would not support the mission effort as Spain had done. The loss to Mission Soledad added to its already burdensome condition. The mission padres and neophytes suffered greatly from the lack of food and starvation. A smallpox epidemic killed hundreds of Native Americans. Many of the Indians believed they were cursed because they had chosen the whiteman's God.

The Mexican Governor sold the mission for $800.00 in 1846. When the United States took control of California, the mission land was returned to the Catholic church in 1859. It was in a ruinous and decayed condition. Finally, in 1955 restoration and reconstruction efforts were begun on the mission.

When the padres built an aqueduct system, transporting water from the Salinas River to the dusty, wind swept earth that surrounded the mission, a transformation took place. The water allowed for crops to flourish and cattle to multiply. Even the neophyte population increased to over 700 people.

Today the mission church has been reconstructed, along with the building that housed the padres' living quarters. Lovely gardens have developed around the mission and in the quadrangle area behind the long building. History is coming alive at Mission Soledad with continued restoration efforts.

In 1824 heavy winter rains brought the waters of the Salinas River over its banks, flooding the valley and destroying the church. Again, in 1828, flood waters destroyed the rebuilt church. For a third time, in 1832, the raging water brought an end to the mission life. In 1834 secularization destroyed what was left of the mission efforts.

In 1791 Manuel Ruiz was hired by the government to design and build the imposing stone-walled structure, which stands today, utilizing his abilities as a master stone mason. The individuality of Mission Carmel is illustrated by its stylish architecture, such as the identifying Moorish dome and the geometric star-designed window that greets its visitor through the ornate *Espandaña,* or false front. Although the roof, created of reeds and large wooden support timbers deteriorated and collapsed under the weight of the tiles in later years, the everlasting stone walls remained. Under the strong leadership of Father Fermin Francisco de Lasuén, the church construction was completed and dedicated in 1797.

Mission San Carlos
Borroméo de Carmelo

1770, Second Mission
3080 Rio Road, Carmel-by-the-Sea, CA 93923

Named for the 16th-century cardinal, St. Charles of Borroméo, Mission San Carlos Borroméo was established on June 3, 1770, on the shore of Monterey Bay by the Spanish Franciscan padre, Fray Junipero Serra. He arrived by ship, the *San Antonio*, from San Diego and met the overland group led by Don Gaspar de Portola who left San Diego in mid-May. The presidio, which housed the Spanish soldiers, and the new mission remained side by side for just a year. The mission was moved to its current site, south to the Carmel Valley along the Carmel River. The move protected the Native Americans from the badgering soldiers. It took six months for the church building to be erected, along with other shelters.

In 1834 the order for secularization of Mission Carmel was announced and this was the beginning of the end of mission life as originally directed by the Viceroy of New Spain. The buildings retained by the church began to deteriorate and soon rubble was all that was left. The stone-walled church became home to rodents, birds and roaming cattle, while wild grasses and weeds flourished inside the building. Restoration efforts began in 1884 with the building of a high-pitched shingle roof, which was an extreme design change from the sloping mounded style of the original tile roof. However, this protective covering maintained the interior protection until 1936, when detailing restoration was begun by Harry W. Downie, considered to be the leading authority on mission architecture and reconstruction. Mission San Carlos Borroméo de Carmelo displays an authentic representation of its original design.

Fray Serra directed mission operations from this mission for 14 years, identifying Carmel as mission headquarters. Upon his death in 1784, Fray Serra's devoted friend, Fr. Palou replaced Serra as President until his retirement in 1785, when Fr. Fermin de Lasuén became the mission's Father-President. Mission authority remained in Carmel up to his death in 1803 when it was transferred to Mission Santa Barbara.

Mission San Juan Bautista

On June 24, 1797, Fr. Fermin de Lasuén chose the site for Mission San Juan Bautista, named in honor of John the Baptist, on a short bluff overlooking the San Benito Valley. Unknowingly, the mission was located next to the infamous San Andreas fault. Immediate efforts were made to construct shelters. Within a few months workmen had erected an adobe church, storehouses, barracks, and a guardhouse. Small adobe houses were built for the Native Americans who converted to mission life.

The Native Americans were curious and friendly. This mix led to successful Christian conversions and accepting the mission way of life. Records indicate that over 500 neophytes were living at the mission by 1800, just three years following its founding. By the time the new church was completed in 1812, the Indian congregation had diminished by over 50% from the high count of 1,100 recorded in 1805. Death and desertion reduced the population. Every effort was used to maintain the Indian's interest. Fr. Estévan Tápis, gifted in musical talent, created a male choir, so enjoyed by the entire congregation and locals. Fr. de la Cuesta was a natural linguist, knowing over a dozen Indian languages. His ability to deliver his Christian teachings in seven different languages was an asset to the missionary efforts. His written works of Indian phrases and the study of the Mutsumi language are regarded as the foundation of insight to the understanding of the ways of the California Native Americans.

In 1834 Governor José Figuero announced the decree for secularization of all the missions. Mission life changed for San Juan Bautista, especially for the Indians. However, throughout the troubled times a padre was always in attendance. The mission became part of the little pueblo community that had developed next to it, known as San Juan Bautista. On November 19, 1859, the United States government returned the mission to the church.

Over the years the "modernizers" have struck this mission, much as was experienced at other missions. In about 1860 a new padre covered the bells with a New England-style steeple, a style lasting well into the 1950s. When visiting San Juan Bautista, one is able to step back to the earlier days of the town and mission, both steeped in history. A state park edges the plaza and mission grounds, providing a glance back to the Gold Rush days. The church can be seen as Father de la Cuesta designed it, with three aisles. The beautifully painted altarpiece, *reredos,* still wears the vivid paint laid down by Thomas Doak, California's first American citizen, and his workmen in the 1820s. Still an active center for religious teachings, the mission is an integral part of the local community, achieving what it set out to do in 1797.

Continued population growth required a larger church facility. A new church was begun in 1803 and dedicated in 1812. Fr. Felipe del Arroyo de la Cuesta arrived in 1808, taking charge of the mission. He made many building revisions, especially in the nave or main body of the church, changing it from the customary one room with a center aisle to a room accommodating three aisles. The room was large enough to handle 1,000 people. After completion fear of potential damage by earthquakes caused the closing of the two side aisles, returning the church interior to its original one-room design.

Saved from the devastating 1812 earthquakes that damaged many of the other missions (the 1812 quakes followed different earth faults), Mission San Juan Bautista received extensive damage during the 1906 earthquake along the San Andreas fault. It crumbled church walls and many of the outer buildings. Over the following years, reconstruction and restoration efforts have brought the church back to its useful purpose. Steel, concrete and heavy cross-bracing have been implemented to reinforce the building's stability.

In 1931 a small replica of the original mission church was constructed, built to honor the heritage of Mission Santa Cruz. The chapel houses statues, paintings, candlesticks, and the tabernacle used during the time the mission was serving the neophyte community. A small museum of memorabilia is present, providing a glimpse into the interesting mission life.

Mission Santa Cruz

There is little evidence of the original Mission Santa Cruz, named for the Sacred Cross and founded on August 28, 1791. Father Fermin de Lasuén selected the site for the mission but did not officiate over the dedication ceremony. The settlement was established swiftly and without problems. So many positive qualities prevailed. The mission had an excellent location site, situated on a hill, commanding a view of the valley and river below. The fertile soil of the area combined with the excellent climate, produced bountiful crops. The Native Americans were an amiable group, eager to participate in the Franciscan endeavors. The first mission church was completed in 1794 and the quadrangle, workshops, storage units, and dormitories were completed in 1795. Millstones brought from Mission Carmel were used to grind the harvested corn and wheat into flour. The padres were fulfilling their obligation to the Native Americans by teaching them creative skills and the way of Christianity.

From the founding of the mission in August, 1791 to October, 1794, the mission padres experienced little if any objections from the ruling governor. Two governors had served during that three-year period, both with relaxed attitudes regarding missions. That unconcerned approach ceased with the arrival of Governor Diego Borica who immediately became a problem for the padres. Borica was charged by the Viceroy to establish a third pueblo in Alta California. Previously, Juan Bautista de Anza established two pueblos near missions: San Francisco de Asis (Dolores) and Santa Clara de Asis. Instead of being the required one Spanish league away from the mission (about 3 miles), the town known as Branciforté was established just across the San Lorenzo River, a very short distance from the mission. Diego Borica made grand plans for the settlement, promoting land development, special housing provisions, and lucrative wages for the colonists he was enticing with his promises. He received people equal to his words: unworthy and meaningless regarding their work ethic and moral values. Most were prone toward an illicit life, had poor health, and an overall lack of ambition. Needless to say, the influence on the neophytes by the citizens was less than gratifying.

The neophyte population began to dwindle, down from a high count of 523 in 1796 to about 300 in 1798, just a two-year period. Newcomers to the settlement encroached on mission land. Fr. Lasuén's complaints were answered with rationalized logic: as the mission neophytes go, so goes the mission's need for the land. (So the townspeople took the land for their use.) This angered the padres who believed swift and harsh punishment to straying neophytes would restrain the wayward converts. This practice caused the murderous death of one priest by seven neophytes who pleaded excessive cruelty by the padre as their defense. They were punished by acts of severe flogging.

In 1818 the governor evacuated the mission when the high-seas pirate, Bouchard, made his appearance in the area. The mission padre asked the Branciforté citizens for help in gathering the valuables of the mission and placing them in safekeeping. This was a mistake. The people merely looted the premises, eating and drinking all they could consume, stealing what was available and damaging the remainder. Upon returning to the mission, the padre experienced so much anger and heartache that he asked for the closure of the mission. His request was denied.

As the town grew in size, the mission dwindled in both dimensions and in neophyte population. Secularization struck hard at the mission. The land, livestock and goods were sold, the building was left to deteriorate, and the Indians moved away. An earthquake in 1857 caused the collapse of the adobe church, rebuilt as a wooden framed building in 1858. The church seen today was constructed in 1889.

Mission Santa Clara de Asis

Lt. Colonel Juan Bautista de Anza led an overland expedition of soldiers, married couples, and pack animals from Sonora, Mexico, to Monterey during the spring of 1776 with the expressed purpose of establishing pueblos, developing two missions and forming a strong presidio near the San Francisco Bay. The first of the two planned missions was Mission San Francisco de Asis, founded in June, 1776, and the second was Mission Santa Clara de Asis, named for Saint Claire of Assissi, Italy, founder of the holy order for nuns, the Poor Claras or Clares. Bautista de Anza had previously chosen a spot near the river he named *Rio de Nuestra Señora de Guadeloupe* for the mission site. He also selected the site of the new pueblo to be nearby, but far enough away from the mission so as not to interfere with mission life. The pueblo was San José.

Departing the San Francisco mission, Lt. Moraga, Fr. Tomás de la Peña, soldiers and some of the families who had emigrated in the spring of 1776 arrived at the Guadeloupe River on January 12, 1777, and established the new mission. The goods brought from Mexico to Monterey for the new mission arrived two weeks later, along with more emigrants, tools, and a few cattle. Mission structures were quickly erected, with the first church built of logs and mud in 1777.

Due to its ideal location in the valley and being near water, the mission's agricultural efforts were heavily rewarded. The fertile land produced bountiful crops. The cattle brought earlier from Monterey developed into an extensive herd. The mingling of the mission cattle with the cattle of the pueblo, San José, created problems for the two units.

The secularization of the mission in 1836 changed life drastically. The land and cattle that belonged to the Indians soon belonged to private citizens. All the attention by the missionaries to help the Native Americans stopped.

When the United States took control of California, a portion of the mission land was returned to the church. Control of Mission Santa Clara was transferred to the Jesuit Order who in 1851 established a college now known as Santa Clara University.

A total of six churches have been built during Santa Clara's existence. Floods, fire, earthquake and time have caused relocation and reconstruction of the buildings. Fr. Murguia designed and supervised the building of the third and most grand, started in 1781 and completed in 1784. Fr. Murguia died just a few days before the building was consecrated by Fray Serra. The fourth church was completed in 1819. The fifth church was really put to the test. Originally completed in 1825, it was remodeled in 1861 and in 1887; it was damaged extensively by fire in 1926 and then dismantled. The building was replaced in 1928 and now maintains its current image.

Though the purpose of the mission was to establish Spanish residence by converting the Native people to Christianity and teaching them Spanish skills of food cultivation and animal husbandry, the government looked upon the mission's purpose as a political one: to stop encroachment by other foreign countries and to use the mission as a resting place for military troops. Both the church and government were successful, even though progress was slow in the beginning and the struggle was ongoing.

The mission buildings began as simple adobe structures. The church building was strong and large. In 1868 that strength was challenged by a massive earthquake that left crumbled walls and a caved-in roof. In 1869 the church was demolished and reconstructed as a wooden framed building. Today a reconstruction of the 1809 church stands at the site.

Mission San José

The need to fill a void was answered by the founding of Mission San José. Wide open spaces and long distances from one protective mission to the next were problems travelers and supply units experienced when traversing from San Diego to the northern mission in San Francisco. It was also necessary to protect the coast settlements from attacks by Indians living in the San Joaquin Valley. Fr. Fermin de Lasuén dedicated Mission San José on June 11, 1797, honoring the earthly father of Jesus, Saint Joseph.

Adobe buildings were erected and mission life was established. During this time conversion of the Native Americans was slow. The local Indians were peaceful and of an independent spirit, many were quite indifferent to the missionary efforts. In spite of this, Native American conversion was extremely successful. By 1831 the neophyte population grew to over 1,870. Between 1797 and the mission secularization in 1834, over 6,700 Indians became Christians, a feat only one other mission surpassed, Mission San Luis Rey. Not only was the mission successful in its Christian teachings, the fathers were excellent teachers of agriculture. Its location on fertile land allowed the mission to excel in fruit and olive production, and its livestock population thrived as well. The mission developed into one of the largest and most successful of the 21 missions.

The government soldiers were also a busy lot protecting the mission as well as protecting supply and exploration units. To the east the sprawling San Joaquin Valley was home to several Native American tribes, some rather hostile. The strategic location of Mission San José seemed to lend itself to be the headquarters for the Indian-fighting soldiers. Many battles involving various Native tribes, north and east of the mission ensued, with casualties on both sides. The San Francisco Presidio sent troops out several times to quell Native uprisings. General Mariano Vallejo, one of the two brothers leaving their mark on the mission's history, guided a successful march against a fighting group of over 500, led by a mission convert, Estanislao, who backed away from his mission teachings.

Father Narciso Duran and Father Buenaventura Fortuni were assigned to Mission San José in 1806. Through their combined efforts, the mission flourished. Fr. Fortuni transferred out in 1826. Father Duran's leadership skills led to his election as Father-President of the California missions from 1825-1827 and from 1831-1838. His success as a music master, although self taught, brought acclaim to the mission. He was so successful in training the converts on musical instruments and reading the music he wrote, that he created a 30-piece orchestra involving trumpets, flutes, violins, violas, and drums, plus having striking uniforms.

Following the order to secularize, Don José Jésus Vallejo was appointed administrator of the mission property, valued at over $150,000. It depreciated rapidly and on May 6, 1846, the entire remaining property was sold by the Mexican government for $12,000. The American military governor, General Kearny, refused to recognize this as a valid sale and ordered the mission property to remain in the hands of the padre-in-charge.

Extensive renovation and reconstruction began in 1982, bringing the mission back to much of the grand image it once possessed. The $5,000,000 project rebuilt a replica of the old mission church which now stands along with an original building in which visitors will find the mission's museum.

Mission San Francisco de Asis

When San Francisco Bay was finally located by Gaspar de Portola in 1769, Spain immediately determined the importance of maintaining its presence in the area. A body of water large enough to "hold all the ships of Spain" gained the attention of the Viceroy who agreed with Fray Serra that missions were necessary to establish Spain's presence. He also wanted a military garrison and a pueblo established. This involved more than the typical two padres and a few soldiers, it would require a major immigration.

Earlier in the year of 1776, Lt. Colonel Juan Bautista de Anza directed a group of 240 people from Sonora, Mexico to Monterey with the expressed purpose of establishing those colonies in the San Francisco Bay area. Married couples, soldiers, pack animals and a thousand head of cattle ventured across vast deserts, torturous mountains, and expansive valleys to reach their destination of Monterey. Once arriving in Monterey, Bautista de Anza and a small party traveled ahead to San Francisco Bay and there he selected sites for the mission, presidio, and pueblo, which he named *Yerba Buena*. The mission would be next to a small lake he named *Laguna de Nuestra Señora de los Dolores* and the small stream feeding the lake was named *Arroyo de los Dolores*, in honor of Our Lady of Sorrow. (It was due to the location near the river and lake that the mission became identified as Mission Dolores.) The Lt. Colonel returned to Monterey and placed Lt. Moraga in charge of the colonizing group destined for the new mission and pueblo. On June 17, 1776, Lt. Moraga, Father Palou, a small group of emigrants and soldiers and the sailing vessel *San Carlos* departed Monterey for the San Francisco Bay. The overland group arrived first and on June 29th Fr. Palou founded Mission San Francisco de Asis, named in honor of St. Francis of Assisi who founded the Franciscan Order, of which the founding padres were members. The ship, which arrived six weeks later on August 18th, carried goods needed for the establishment of the mission, presidio, and pueblo.

Missionary success was exemplary despite the hurdles experienced by the missionary fathers. The weather was a major contributor to the dilemma. Heavy fog, penetrating dampness, piercing rain and wind made living in the area a hardship. Records indicate over 4,000 Native Americans converted to Christianity, yet mission life was not their first choice. Agricultural crops did not prosper as they did with other missions. Work demands were often unheeded. Health problems were severe. Unable to cope with the white man's sicknesses, illness and death prevailed. In 1817 a mission hospital was established north, across the Bay, where warm sunshine and a drier environment worked miracles on the health of the people. The hospital was known as San Rafael. Secularization in 1834 brought the decline of the mission. The city surrounded the mission, bringing a much "faster" lifestyle to the area. By 1845 the mission was sold to the private sector, but in 1847 the property was returned to the Catholic church by Presidential proclamation.

Saved from church "modernizers", the original mission church appears very much as it did in its early years. Nestled next to the massive parish church and surrounded by apartment buildings of varied architectural designs, little Mission Dolores still maintains it strength of valor and the respect of the community.

The first church was built of wood and mud with tule reeds used for the roof. In 1791 Fr. Palou dedicated a new church, relocated away from the lake, a more desirous location. Today's church is much the same as the exquisite structure of 1791. The acreage diminished due to the encroachment of civilization. The simple structures involved with the mission have all disappeared. The beautiful basilica located next to the original chapel was built to be the parish church, replacing the small chapel. The earthquake of 1906 caused such severe structural damage that the church was dismantled. The rebuilding efforts were not completed until 1918. The old chapel of Mission Dolores was not damaged during the earthquake of 1906 or during the more recent temblor of 1989.

Father Gil y Toboada built a plain, straightforward building with a multi-purpose use: a chapel, priest quarters, small shops, and the infirmary. The building, completed in 1818, was 87 feet long and 42 feet wide. Today's replica includes a star window that was not part of the original church. This design came from the imagination of a postcard artist who felt the mission needed something more interesting than the standard rectangular window. Perhaps the artist had previously visited Mission Carmel where the star-designed window was used.

Mission San Rafael, Arcangel

1817, Twentieth Mission
1104 Fifth Avenue, San Rafael, CA 94901

Mission San Rafael was established as a hospital to care for the sick neophytes from Mission San Francisco de Asis, or more commonly referred to as Mission Dolores. The white man's illnesses brought death to many. The damp, foggy weather and the heavy rains and wind added to chronic health and fatigue problems. It was difficult to be warm and dry.

Father Ramón Abella of Mission Dolores explained to Governor Sola the need for assistance for his sick people. The governor learned of an ideal location a few miles north of San Francisco Bay where warm, sunny days and an overall drier climate prevailed. The area was protected from the strong, cold winds by mountains and rolling hills. The Native Americans in the area were friendly. Conditions were perfect for establishing an assistant location for Mission Dolores and permission was granted by the government and the church. On December 13, 1817, Father Vincenti de Sarría, Father Gil y Toboada, who volunteered to oversee the medical care, and several other padres crossed the Bay and journeyed north to the selected site of the hospital. Fr. Sarría said the first mass for the new *asistencia* on December 14, naming the hospital in honor or Saint Rafael, the Arcangel, patron saint to the healing arts. Though not identified as a mission, nonetheless 200 local Native Americans presented themselves for religious instruction and 26 Native children were baptized before the founding ceremonies were concluded.

The sunshine did wonders to return health and to bring comfort to the suffering neophytes. Soon other missions sent their sick to the *asistencia*. The local Indians also came to San Rafael seeking religious guidance. Though not planned, San Rafael was elevated to mission stature in 1823.

In 1819 Father Juan Amoros succeeded Fr. Gil. He was the guiding light for mission success. By 1828 the neophyte population grew to 1,140. The kind, understanding padre led the Indians to a rewarding life, teaching them the ways to self-sufficiency. When Father Amoros died, after 13 years of dedicated service, a more gregarious, perhaps clashing priest led the mission, Father José Maria Mercado. He was always very protective of the mission and its Indian population. He even clashed with General Mariano Vallejo, whom he believed was exploiting the Native Americans. Life was not always calm at the mission.

Mission San Rafael was the first of the missions to be secularized in 1834. General Mariano Vallejo was appointed official administrator. He immediately set about confiscating mission land and goods from the Indians, who received shares of land at the time of secularization. He removed livestock, interior and exterior furnishings, farm implements, and even the grape vines and fruit trees to his own large ranch properties. By 1842 the mission was abandoned. In 1855 the U.S. government returned the mission to the Catholic church. With the lack of maintenance the adobe buildings deteriorated. By 1861 the mission structures were torn down to salvage the wood. A new parish church was built.

Today's chapel constructed in 1949 on the approximate site to the first chapel, is a replica of the original little church built by Father Gil in 1818. There is no record regarding the original decor of the first church. What is displayed is appropriate to the time.

Mission San Francisco Solano

Father José Altimira was assigned to Mission Dolores in 1819. He was extremely dissatisfied with the conditions at Mission Dolores and believed the only solution to the problems experienced at the mission was to close it down and move to a new location. The problem was twofold: miserable weather and sick people. He was aware of Mission San Rafael and its success, however he believed Mission San Rafael should be closed also. He wanted to move everything to a new location, farther north and inland from Mission San Rafael. He by-passed the proper church authorities who made such decisions and took his idea to Governor Don Luis Arguello. He agreed with Fr. Altimira that Mission Dolores did have miserable conditions and it should be closed, along with San Rafael. The idea was activated by the civil authorities without the church knowing of the plans. When Father-President Señan received the news about the new mission, he was explosively angry and reprimanded both Governor Arguello and Father Altimira. After many negotiations between the two factions, the civil authorities and the church, Fr. Altimira was given permission to found the mission, with the understanding that neither Mission Dolores nor San Rafael would close. On July 4, 1823, Mission San Francisco Solano was founded, the last of the California missions to be established.

The first church, a temporary wooden structure, began in 1823 and was completed in 1824. Dedication services were held on April 4th. Father-President Señan instructed Father Altimira to name the mission in honor of Peruvian missionary Francis Solano. Many other buildings were completed that year also: workshops, a granary, barracks for the soldiers, a guardhouse, and a tile-roofed monastery. After all the work and effort Fr. Altimira put into his mission, his success with the neophytes was poor. He used flogging and imprisonment as control methods. In 1826 an angry group of Indians invaded the mission, looting and burning their way through the compound. Father Altimira was so disheartened by the actions of the Indians that he requested a transfer to another mission. His request was accepted and Father Buenaventura Fortuni was given the position. Fr. Fortuni restored the mission both physically and spiritually. He built a large new adobe church and enlarged the *convento* to accommodate 27 rooms. Father Fortuni guided the mission to a prosperous position. The neophytes farmed over 10,000 acres, producing abundant crops and strong livestock. The neophyte population grew to 996. Fr. Fortuni left the mission after seven years of devoted service.

In 1834 General Mariano Vallejo was appointed commandant of the northern frontier and later commissioner of the mission following the secularization law. Unable to manage their land, General Vallejo moved the Indians to his ranch where they lived and worked. The general developed the pueblo of Sonoma so he could bring soldiers to the area from the San Francisco Presidio to maintain order and to provide protection from outside factions. The buildings deteriorated rapidly. By 1881 the mission was sold. A new parish church was built elsewhere in Sonoma.

The museum located in the old mission buildings provides an insight to the mission life and into the Sonoma area. The small adobe chapel, restored to an authentic appearance, opens its doors to all visitors. The quadrangle has flowers and trees and waits patiently for happy voices. Only five of the original 27 buildings stand today next to the quadrangle.

In 1903 the land was purchased by the Historic Landmark League. The buildings that remained on the property were in desperate condition. The 1906 earthquake added to the repair problems. The church, which was badly damaged, was restored by 1912. The League deeded the property to the state of California in 1926. During 1943 and 1944 the state provided the necessary funds for further restoration. Today, the mission is part of the State Park System.